First published in the Federal
Republic of Germany 1987
by Ravensburger Buchverlag
First published in Great Britain 1989
by Victor Gollancz Ltd
14 Henrietta Street, London WC2E 8QJ

© 1987 by Ravensburger Buchverlag Otto Maier GmbH
Original German title: *Ich Mach Was Mit Knete*

British Library Cataloguing in Publication Data
Lohf, Sabine
   Things I make with modelling clay
   1. Modelling in clay. For children
   I. Title
   731.4'2

ISBN 0-575-04542-6

Printed in the Federal Republic of Germany

Sabine Lohf

Things I make with modelling clay

What can you make?

LONDON • VICTOR GOLLANCZ LTD • 1989

Making Figures from Rolled-Out Clay

Making a Snake

Alphabet Letters

Rolling and Cutting Out

Roll the modelling clay flat with a rolling-pin.

Rolling and Pressing Out

Using a Garlic Press

Plait some pigtails
out of spaghetti hair

Sticking Things In

Sticking Things On

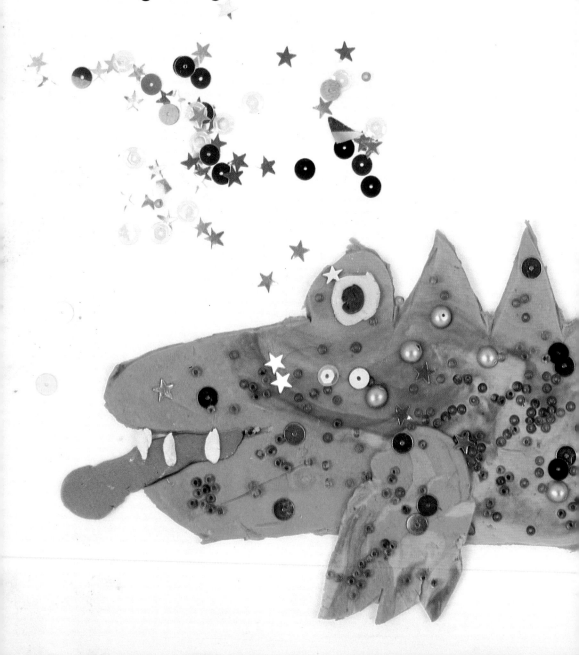

Making Pictures

They look best if you frame them.

Using Leaves and Bark

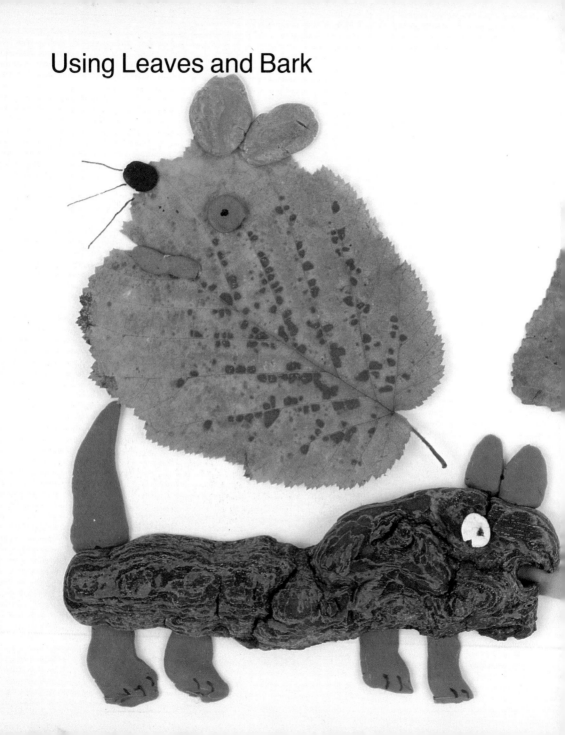

Making Fruit and Vegetables

Lots of Animals

I wanted to make an owl, too. Perhaps I'll do it tomorrow.